WILL ROGERS
- for -
PRESIDENT

An insightful interview featuring thoughts, quotes & anecdotes
of Will Rogers on important election issues

— —

By
CHARLEY GREEN

Copyright © 2008, 2012 by Charles R. Green

ISBN 978-0-9760812-2-7

Published by: C.R. Green & Associates

Will Rogers portrait and photographs courtesy of the

Will Rogers Memorial Museum

1720 West Will Rogers Blvd.

Claremore, Oklahoma 74017

(800) 324-9455

www.WillRogers.com

Illustrations by Jack Wells, Western Artist

Studio & Hideout

1830 Markwell Ave.

Oklahoma City, OK 73127

(405) 789-3920

Additional art work by Kelly Killough, Western Artist

www.kellykilloughstudios.com

Book design by The Creative Department, Inc., Kansas City, MO

www.ideaville.net

www.CharleyGreen.com

AUTHOR'S NOTE

THE CONSIDERATION of Will Rogers as a candidate for President of the United States in 1928 was really a symbolic gesture acknowledging his spirit, insight and honesty. Will had the ability to accurately interpret the political and economic events of the day, events which in many ways relate to our own upcoming elections. His humor, with an occasional sarcastic remark thrown in, kept folk's attention and gave them a reason to stay informed.

As Mr. Rogers' self-appointed Senior Advisor, I've been guided to reiterate his position, views and opinions on what are considered important issues in the upcoming campaign. A little poetic license has been taken and brought into play, utilizing an interview format. The topics are introduced by a question, then answered with one of Candidate Rogers' insightful *Thoughts, Quotes & Anecdotes* in understandable terms and concepts that make sense. Common sense.

Enjoy the timeless sayings and expressions of Will Rogers presented in this book. My goal is to put a smile on your face, provide some insight into the ever-changing (and in many ways, never-changing) world of *Elections & Politics*.

I must give special thanks to the Staff of the Will Rogers Memorial Museum in Claremore, Oklahoma for their assistance and support with these books.

CONTENTS

5 POLITICS & THE WORLD

INTRODUCTION

THE MAN, WILL ROGERS
1879–1935

Will Rogers had a remarkable career that went from Oklahoma "cowpuncher" to international star. He embodied the heart and soul of this nation at a time when a fresh voice, clear eyes and spoken truth were needed. This simple, plain-spoken man, who was part Cherokee Indian and a former cowboy, became the voice of a nation during the '20s and '30s.

His writings, quotes and speaking engagements were directed toward the political arena, as well as other events of the time. Strange as it seems, most of those pearls of wisdom are just as relevant today as they were in Will's day. It is my intent to give readers a point of reference that may apply to some political happening today, as well as a useable quote you may toss out to liven up a conversation or speech.

Will Rogers became the voice of the common man, spending a great deal of his time engaged in conversation with people on the street, regardless of their station in life. He spoke with waitresses, cowboys, farmers, performers and anyone who represented the average person trying to make a living: the people working at doing the right thing, honoring their responsibilities and commitments.

Will liked people and never forgot his roots. He was able to connect with folks in a way most politicians, heads of states and those in high places could not. In many cases, politicians were more interested in their own AGENDA instead of the people who helped get them elected. Some things haven't changed and it seems as if certain principles are embedded in our political system for all times.

Through his message and style of delivery, Will conveyed to the entire nation what was really going on in the heart of the country. As a result of his ability to connect with people and his passion for values and principles, Rogers was accepted, respected, trusted and honored throughout the world, from common men to royalty.

Illustration courtesy of The Will Rogers Memorial Museum

He was intensely inquisitive about life and people. Will traveled extensively, constantly gathering information about the world he experienced. He was a prolific reader and could cut through verbiage quickly, thereby reducing it to understandable terms and concepts that made sense.

The intent of this book is to present a quick read and reference in interview format. Will's timeless philosophy, as well as his insights into political life from yesteryear, is presented as they apply to today's events. These golden nuggets and guiding thoughts will be something you can relate to, learn from, and share with others — possibly opening up certain areas for cussing or discussing.

Will Rogers' Thoughts, Quotes & Anecdotes on Important Election Issues

Will Rogers was an equal opportunity humorist and there weren't many sacred cows left without his brand. So if you feel your political party is being stepped on, just wait a bit. The other person's party will get its fair share of attention shortly. Let's begin.

Will's spelling and style of writing in this book are completely his own. Once admonished about using "ain't," he said, "I know a lot of people who don't say 'ain't ain't eating." When someone else suggested to Will that his syntax was not always appropriate, Will replied, "When I write 'em I am through with 'em. I am not being paid reading wages."

1

CAMPAIGNS
— & —
CANDIDATES

THE CANDIDATES

There are a great many people entering this year's presidential race. Should we assume these folks are qualified to hold the office of the President of the United States?

Anyhow, now there is the early-bird variety of candidates for president. You see we have all these senators in there, all of whom think they are only there till the next election, when they will move to the other end of Pennsylvania Avenue. There will be dozens and dozens come in, mostly through starvation, and partly through thinking that the Democrats can win with practically nothing. And there will be some enter the race that will qualify for nothing. And all the speeches you hear are just preludes to the next presidential elections.

Of course, this early in the game you don't have to offer any constructive remedy. Just to shout what is wrong is enough, and it's all in the game. In fact, the Democrats can call a man more things than the Republicans. Cause there has been so much more that they had practice at.

Denouncing is not only an art with the Democrats, but it's a profession. But for what little practice the Republicans have had, why, they are not doing bad at all. They, for amateur denouncers, are doing fine and may soon be as good as the Democratic denouncers.

Candidates talk about running a "clean campaign." Just what is a "clean campaign?"

A clean campaign is one where each side cleans the other of every possible vestige of respectability.

Does an honest man make the best candidate for public office?

Shrewdness in Public life all over the world is always honored, while honesty in Public Men is generally attributed to Dumbness and is seldom rewarded.

Illustration by Jack Wells, Western artist

Is it true, as some candidates are telling us, that we are facing a critical time in the world's affairs?

Did you ever know a candidate that was not facing 'a most critical time in the world's affairs' every time he spoke in public? I don't know what could be so 'critical'? The world is going along as usual, having about the usual quota of wars, robberies, and murders.

Do the Democrats have a good candidate?

The Democrats not only have a good candidate, but they got money, which it's better to have than a good candidate.

Half of each party is not really crazy about what their candidate stands for, but he stands the best chance of election, and that's the main thing to stand for.

Every candidate seems to have a slogan to make him stand out from the other guy. What will be your position on this issue?

We are going to try and eliminate slogans. Slogans have been more harmful to the country than Bo-Weevil, Luncheon Clubs, Sand Fleas, Detours, Conventions and Golf Pants.

It seems a couple of comedians have declared themselves as candidates for political office in the upcoming elections. Do you think the voters will take them seriously?

I certainly know that a comedian can only last until he either takes himself serious or his audience takes him serious, and I don't want either of those to happen to me until I am dead (if then).

Everything is changing. People are taking their comedians seriously, and the politicians as a joke, when it used to be vice versa.

There's a lot of talk among the candidates about "restoring confidence" in our economy. Can this be done?

Give me some idea where 'confidence' is, and just what you want it restored to. Rich men who never had a mission in life outside of watching a stock ticker are working day and night 'restoring confidence.'

I discovered confidence hasn't left this country. Confidence just got wise and the guys it got wise to are wondering where it has gone.

What are you doing to restore confidence?

I have joined the great movement of Restoring Confidence. There is a lot of people who got Confidence, but they are careful who they have it in. We have plenty of Confidence in this country, but we are a little short of good men to place our Confidence in.

How trustworthy are the promises political candidates make to the voters?

So many Republicans have promised things and then didn't make good that it's getting so a Republican promise isn't much more to be depended on than a Democratic one, and that has always been the lowest form of collateral in the world.

Several important issues are before the American public today, however, it seems candidates are trying to straddle those issues, going for the vote, rather than standing on their convictions and the desires of their constituents.

Ain't it wonderful to have something come up in a country, where you can find out just how many political cowards there are?

In order to get in there, either one [candidate] will promise the voters anything from perpetual motion to eternal salvation.

Illustration by Jack Wells, Western artist

CAMPAIGN FINANCING

Running for political office requires a huge amount of campaign financing. Does this mean the American public is receiving its money's worth?

So much money is being spent on the campaigns that I doubt if either man [or woman], as good as they are, are worth what it will cost to elect them.

Politics has got so expensive that it takes lots of money to even get beat nowadays.

Where do you see your support coming from?

Now a word to the Republican voters, we won't be able to pay you anything for your votes, so that will naturally eliminate all Republican support. And as we can't pay the Democrats, they will naturally, if they have to vote for nothing, stay with their own Party, for they have been voting for nothing for years. So offhand it's hard to see where our support is coming from.

I can't decide which party to make a campaign contribution to. What would you suggest?

Take your campaign contribution, and send it to the Red Cross, and let the election be decided on merit.

CAMPAIGN PROMISES

Is it true that after a politician has been in office for a time, we often forget the campaign promises that were made?

We can get all lathering at the time over some political campaign promise, or some conference pledge, but if the thing just drags along long enough we forget what it was that was originally promised. The short memories of the American voter is what keeps our politicians in office.

Is the way a politician acts in public the same as he does in real life?

When you are in politics and depending on somebody to keep you in, you really ain't able to act like real life. Politicians will use any means to get their cause launched; a funeral, a commemoration, a christening, any occasion that looks important, they will decide to launch along with the chaplain's benediction some of the promises the future holds for you.

NATIONAL CONVENTIONS

What purpose does the Democratic and Republican Conventions serve today?

Our National Conventions are nothing but glorified Mickey Mouse cartoons, and are solely for amusement purposes.

How important is drafting a platform in helping a nominee get elected?

As for drafting a platform, that's a lot of applesauce. Why, I bet you, there is not a Republican or Democratic officeholder today that can tell you one plank in the last election platform, without looking over the minutes.

How does the Democratic platform differ from the Republican platform?

It favors fixing everything the Republicans have ruined, and keeping everything that they haven't.

What could the Democrats have done to make their platform more straight forward so folks really knew where they stood on the issues?

Democrats could have saved forty-two pages of the forty-five page 1924 Democratic platform and perhaps their election if they had come out in the open on every question and told just where they stood.

When you straddle a thing, it takes a long time to explain it.

Have you witnessed any insight coming from someone attending one of the National Conventions?

There was a delegate with his little boy standing beside me on the floor of the convention, and I heard the little fellow ask his daddy: 'Is that man praying for the convention?' And his daddy told him: 'No son! He took one look at the convention, and he's praying for the country.'

These acceptance speeches by the nominees seem to promise a lot. Should we believe what they are saying?

If we got one-tenth of what was promised to us in these acceptance speeches, there wouldn't be any inducement to go to Heaven.

THE NOMINATION

Mr. Rogers, is there a good reason why you should be considered as a candidate for President of these United States?

The hour demands a leader. The voice of the people calls. Who am I that I should hesitate?

This is a very serious moment in the destinies of the nation. The Democratic Party is locked in a stranglehold and can make no progress. My candidacy represents nothing more than the effort of the plain people — of which I am one — to remedy this disastrous condition of affairs.

It is my duty to go directly to the scene of the conflict and marshal the forces of right and justice. I do not seek this office, but respond to public demand.

Another big reason why I should be nominated is I am a Democrat. Another still bigger reason why I should be nominated is I am not a Republican. I am just progressive enough to suit the dissatisfied. And lazy enough to be a Stand Patter.

What qualities should be considered for any man seeking this nomination?

I think any fair-minded man will give me serious consideration.

They have got to nominate a farmer who understands the farmers' condition. I got two farms in Oklahoma, both mortgaged, so no man knows their condition more than I do.

He has to be a man of the West. Well, if a man came from 25 feet further West than I lived last year, he would have to be a fish in the Pacific Ocean.

Is humility an admirable trait in a presidential candidate?

Every candidate always says 'why, there is dozens of men that is more competent to fill this office than I am.'

Well I don't feel that way about it at all. It looks like you boys was inspired when you made your choice. For after all it's only the office of Candidate that I am accepting. You know it don't take near as good a man to be Candidate as it does to hold the office. That's why we wisely defeat more than we elect.

What is your campaign strategy?

My plan of campaign is to go along until all the other candidates have begun to show signs of weakening — about Labor Day — then throw in my reserve.

We shall make a brief whirlwind campaign. That is the way we have started. I already explained how my vote has practically doubled without me turning a hand.

When we throw in the reserve, that will make three of us. We will be as obstinate as the rest of them.

Now this whole acceptance is based on one thing: if elected I absolutely and positively agree to resign. That's my only campaign pledge or slogan, elect Rogers and he will resign.

That's offering the country more than any candidate ever offered it in the entire history of its existence.

How do you think women will react to your candidacy?

We may alienate the entire female vote, but there will be no effort for sex appeal. Of course, if it unconsciously manifests itself, we can't help it.

If you receive the nomination, will you promise the American people more than the other candidates?

No matter what the other side promises, [we'll] see their promise and raise 'em two more.

Every major candidate has a platform. What will your platform advocate?

Our platform will be, whatever the other fellow don't do, we will. No man would want a broader, or more numerous planked platform than that.

There will also be no promise of jobs, for no defeated candidate has ever been able to give anyone a job,

Our support will have to come from those who want nothing, and have the assurance of getting it.

No matter what's on our Platform, on November 5 we will have a bonfire and burn the platform. We are only drafting it for election purposes.

Which political party are you affiliated with?

I am not a member of any organized party — I'm a Democrat.

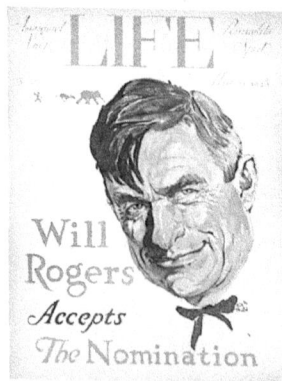

Life magazine has endorsed your candidacy with the following editorial and cover:

Life Magazine Cover, May 31, 1928 launching the campaign of Will Rogers for President as the Anti-Bunk Party candidate.

"In a quiet way, we have been searching for a bunkless candidate who would run for the Presidency on an honest, courageous and reasonably intelligent platform.

"We have been conducting a private straw poll to ascertain whether anyone believed such a candidate was possible. The question which we asked was this: If you could cast aside all party prejudice, who would be your ideal choice for President?

"The answer, from a large group of representative Americans, took the form of an overwhelming majority for Will Rogers.

"And why not?

"Will Rogers, to begin with, is an American. Equipped as he is with a generous supply of genuine Indian blood, he's a lot closer to 100% American than are most of the people who brag about it.

"In the second place, Will Rogers is a humorist. If elected, he would be the first President in sixty-two years who was funny intentionally.

"In the third place, Will Rogers has had wider experience as a public servant than any man that has ever run for office. Not only has he been mixed up in politics (he has served as Mayor of Beverly Hills, Cal., he has been designated 'Congressman at large,' and he holds the commission of Colonel in Kentucky); he is also a veteran of thirteen campaigns in the Ziegfeld Follies.

"In the fourth place, Will Rogers has seen something of the world. He knows more about our foreign relations than do all the eighteen august members of the Senatorial Foreign Relations Committee. He was famous as an Ambassador of Good Will when Lindbergh was still toting mail between St. Louis and Chicago.

"In the fifth place, Will Rogers is a good scout — and it's just about time that the people of the United States of America elected a president for no other reason than that.

"There will be objections to Will Rogers' candidacy. Indeed, most of the qualifications mentioned above would be enough to disqualify him under the rules which usually obtain in politics.

"For instance: the fact that he has set foot on foreign soil, and has made friends with Englishmen, Russians, Mexicans and similar undesirables, will be used by many as a serious argument in his disfavor.

"The fact that he is a comedian will also hurt him, beyond all questions of doubt. The American voters like to laugh at their politicians, not with them.

"Will Rogers accordingly was offered the nomination for the Presidency, as representative of a party which is dedicated to only one supreme purpose; 'To fight Bunk in all its forms.'"

In addition, Henry Ford, the automobile magnate stated:

"The joke of Will Rogers' candidacy for President is that it is no joke. It is a serious attempt to restore American common sense to American politics."

How do you react to these endorsements?

It leaves me dazed and if I can stay dazed I ought to make a splendid candidate.

Since you make your living outside politics, do you think this will affect your support from other politicians?

I admit I can make a living outside politics. Now when you admit that you can live without depending on politics, you lose right there the support of all politicians.

ELECTIONS

As elections are fast approaching, what do you think the results will show when they're over?

A flock of Democrats will replace a mess of Republicans in quite a few districts. It won't mean a thing. They will go in like all the rest of 'em; go in on promises and come out on alibis.

Do the politicians really know how the American Public is going to vote in the upcoming elections?

There is one thing you can bet on this year. No voter is going to do anything that a politician thinks he will do. The way most people feel, they would like to vote against all of 'em, if it was possible.

What is the real issue in this election?

I have been trying to read the papers and see just what it is in this election that one party wants that the other one don't. To save my soul, I can't find any difference. The only thing that I can see where they differ is that the Democrats want the Republicans out and let them in, and the Republicans don't want to get out. That, right there is the issue.

Do we really need elections?

Elections is just what we need. We don't know what we need 'em for, but it's for something, if only to get one-half of our folks sore at the other half.

Isn't each political party trying to look their best during the elections?

With elections coming on, both sides are going to put their best side forward. They are just trying to figure out which side is their best.

What can you compare an election to?

Elections are really a good deal like marriages, there's no accounting for anyone's taste. Every time you see a bridegroom, we wonder why she picked him, and it's the same with public officials.

Do politicians, money and elections have anything in common?

When there is money in an election, it's always in doubt

America has the best politicians money can buy.

Do the voters in the primary election really determine the nominations?

The poor fellow voting in the primary still takes it seriously and really thinks he has something to do with the nominations.

Illustration courtesy of The Will Rogers Memorial Museum

2

THE
POLITICAL
SYSTEM

POLITICAL PARTY DIFFERENCES

Are the Democratic and Republican Parties necessary to run our country?

I tell you, this country runs in spite of parties. In fact, parties are the biggest handicap we have to contend with. If we didn't have to stop to play politics, any administration could almost make a Garden of Eden out of us. You could transfer the Congress over to run Standard Oil, or General Motors, and they'd have both things bankrupt in two years. No other business in the world could afford to carry such deadwood.

Which political party does the most good when it is in control of Congress?

I generally give the Party in Power, whether Republican or Democrat, the more digs because they are generally doing the Country the most damage, and besides, I don't think it is fair to jump too much on the fellow who is down. He is not working, he is only living in hopes of getting back in on the graft in another four years.

What do you see as some of the key differences between the Political Parties?

You know, every year it gets harder and harder to tell the difference between a Republican and a Democrat — course, outside of looks. Their platforms and policies become more and more alike.

But I believe I have found out the sure way to tell one from another this year. It's just the way they talk. The Republicans say, "Well, things could have been worse!" And the Democrats say, "How?"

Illustration by Jack Wells, Western artist

I don't know why it is, but Democrats just seem to have an uncanny premonition of sizing up a question, and guessing wrong on it. It almost makes you think sometimes it is done purposely. You can't make outsiders believe it's not done purposely, for they don't think people could make that many mistakes accidentally.

Republicans have a certain foresight and take over the reins of government about the time things are going good. And when they see pestilence and famine about to visit on the land, they will slip it back to the Democrats.

The Republican candidate says: 'The majority of the country is prosperous.' He means by that that the Republicans are prosperous, and he kinder insinuates that if a man don't know enough to be a Republican, then how can he expect to know enough to be prosperous?

Democrats could live on little, because they never had anything else. But they sure don't live on little when they get into office.

The Republicans have always been the party of big business. The Democrats of small business. So you just take your pick. The Democrats have their eye on a dime and the Republicans on a dollar.

The Republican and the Democratic parties both split. The Republicans have their splits right after election, and the Democrats have their just before an election.

What is the political strategy of the Democrats and the Republicans?

Democrats are attacking and the Republicans are defending. All the Democrats have to do is promise what they would do if they got in. But the Republicans have to promise what they would do and then explain WHY they haven't already done it.

Are there any noticeable differences between Senators of different parties?

There is nothing in the world as alike as two senators. No matter how different their politics, how different the parts of the country they come from, they all look alike, think alike and want alike.

What do you consider to be the #1 problem with the Democratic Party today?

The trouble with the Democrats up to now has been that they have been giving the people 'what they thought the people ought to have' instead of what the people wanted.

How do you feel about Republicans?

There ain't any finer folks living than a Republican that votes the Democratic ticket.

There is something about a Republican that you can only stand him just so long; and on the other hand, there is something about a Democrat that you can't stand him quite that long.

How do you feel about Democrats?

Democrats — you can't shame them into even dying. They would keep on living just to spite the Republicans.

Their greatest trait to recommend the Democrats is optimism and humor. You've got to be an optimist to be a Democrat, and you've got to be a humorist to stay one.

Democrats never agree on anything, that's why they are Democrats. If they agreed with each other, they would be Republicans.

Illustration by Jack Wells, Western artist

CONGRESS & SENATE

What does it mean when Congress talks about amending the Constitution?

It means that the men who drew up this thing years ago didn't know much, and we are just now getting a bunch of real fellows who can take the old parchment and fix it up like it should have been all these years. An I guess, when they get the Constitution all fixed up, they'll start in on the Ten Commandments, just as soon as they'll find somebody in Washington who has read them.

Is Congress concerned about today's high cost of living?

I see a committee down in Washington, who were investigating the high cost of living, turned in their report. [It read] 'we find the cost of living very high, and we recommend more funds to carry on the investigation.'

Mr. Rogers, when it comes to appropriations, how well are our Congressmen and senators doing?

I went down to Washington a couple of times to see what our hired help was doing. They was just appropriating right and left. The U.S. Treasury to them is just a rainbow, there is no end to it.

You see, appropriations for the boys back home is what gets you the votes. Putting on taxes to get the money to appropriate is a sure way to lose votes, So everybody is handing it out, and nobody has the nerve to replenish what they are taking out. Those birds, naturally, have an eye for their own employment.

Every little, old one-cylinder senator and punctured-tired Congressman from all over the country is trying to put over his little local scheme. You know, that's the sad part about politics.

Illustration by Jack Wells, Western artist

These are the men that will get elected every time, the ones that are able to hornswoggle the government out of something for some kind of scheme, just for his own district's special benefit. Any man that looked after the interests of the majority in politics, why, he wouldn't even be nominated the second time. He has got to come in with some loot from somewhere. And the more he drags in, the more solid he is at the next election.

I tell you, if it was in private life, and he put over some of the polite banditry that he does in official life, he would be caught and sent to jail, instead of back to Congress. And then they wonder why our real big men never go into politics.

Does any branch of the government use slogans?

Even Congress has slogans:

Why sleep at home when you can sleep in Congress?

Be a politician, no training necessary!

Join the senate and investigate something!

Come to Washington and vote to raise your pay!

Who should I contact if I want to make my views heard in Congress?

Write to your congressman. Even if he can't read, write to him.

Mr. Rogers, I understand you've kept a diary of the United States Senate about the ways they are trying to find money they've already spent, to finance programs. What is their agenda to raise this money?

Monday — Soak the rich.

Tuesday — Begin hearing from the rich.

Tuesday afternoon — Decide to give the rich a chance to get richer.

Wednesday — Tax Wall Street sales.

Thursday — Get word from Wall Street: lay off us or you will get no campaign contributions.

Friday — Soak the little fellow.

Saturday — Find out there is no little fellow. He has been soaked till he drowned.

Sunday — Meditate.

Next week, same procedure, only more talk and less results.

THE PRESIDENT

What do you believe the American Public wants in a President?

Republicans want a man that can lend dignity to the office.

Democrats want a man that will lend some money.

How important is it for the President to have competent advisors?

I have always maintained that NO President can be as bad as the men that advise him.

An example:

I was up at the White House today. Do you want me to tell you the latest political jokes, Mr. President? I ask him.

"You don't have to, Will," he said; "I know 'em already. I appointed most of them."

Sometimes we don't need a different man as bad as we need different advisors for the same man.

Do presidents have a plan when they take office?

Most of our presidents never went in much for plans. They only had one plan that said: Boys, my head is turned; just get it while you can.

Does it seem like some presidents are long on courage, but short on ability and skills to properly govern the United States?

It's not a disgrace not to be able to run a country nowadays, but it is a disgrace to keep on trying when you know you can't.

3

POLITICIANS
– & –
POLITICKING

HONESTY & TRUTH

Is there really such a thing as truth in politics?

If you ever injected truth into politics, you would have no politics.

What do you think is the real reason someone would want to run for public office?

Nowadays all a man goes into public office for is so he can try to find out something, then write a book about it when he comes out.

THE LIMELIGHT

How has all the TV programming, both network and cable, affected the publicity that politicians are able to generate today?

It seems politicians clamor to be before the cameras if there's a chance for some publicity.

Personally, I think the camera has done more harm for politics than any other one faction. Everybody would rather get their picture in the paper [now TV] than their ideas.

There is no other line of business that any of them could get in where they would get one-tenth part of the publicity that they get in public office, and how they love it. Talk about actors basking in the limelight! Say, an old senator can make an actor look like he is hid under a barrel.

Illustration by Jack Wells, Western artist

POLITICAL SPEECH, ADVICE & DEBATES

What impact does a politician's speech have upon the average voter?

There is not a voter in America that twenty-four hours after any speech could remember two sentences in it. Politics amuse more people than they interest.

WOMEN IN POLITICS

Mr. Rogers, do you see women having a significant role in our political system?

It won't be no time until some woman will become so desperate politically and lose all prospectus of right and wrong and maybe go from bad to worse and finally wind up in the Senate.

Men gave 'em the vote and never meant for them to take it seriously. But being women they took the wrong meaning and did.

Women promised us that if they had the vote, they would clean up politics. About all they have added to the whole voting and political thing is just more votes and more bookkeeping. But it ain't the women's fault. Politics is bigger than any race and it's bigger than any sex.

Can a woman be effective in international affairs?

It's no joking matter getting the world to disarm. Maybe a woman can do it. It's a cinch men can't.

Illustration by Jack Wells, Western artist

Have women's voting rights made any real changes in our political system?

It has! It has doubled the number of candidates.

Do women want some of the same things men seek in politics?

Women voters, do you think they are a-buying 'Glorious Traditions' at the polls? No, sir! They want to know what kind of break they are going to get in Commerce and Industry. If they are going to make the living for the family, they want to know what kind of inducement the government is going to make to them for doing it.

Are women stronger than most men give them credit for?

Women are not the weak, frail, little flowers that they are advertised. There has never been anything invented yet, including war, that a man would enter into, that a woman wouldent, too.

What do Democratic and Republican women want?

Democratic women want birth control of Republicans and Republican women want equal corruption for both sexes.

Are we getting closer to true equality of the sexes?

I'll bet you the time ain't far off when a woman won't know any more than a man.

— 🎩 —

INTELLECT, POLITICIANS & VOTERS

In the eyes of a president, how smart does he think politicians are, anyway?

Roosevelt said he would take brains anytime in preference to politics. He just as good as admitted you couldn't get both in the same body.

Do the candidates intentionally try to impress voters with how smart they are?

Of all the bunk handed out during a campaign, the biggest is to flatter the intelligence of the voters. How are the voters going to be any smarter when the candidates themselves are no smarter?

Does a lack of knowledge help or hurt a candidate's chances?

It isn't what we don't know that gives us trouble, it's what we know that ain't so.

Is it true many voters don't take much time to decide on which candidate or issue to vote for?

When a fellow ain't got much mind, it don't take him long to make it up.

Is it true the American people are very forgiving?

The American people are a very generous people; they will forgive almost any weakness, with the possible exception of stupidity.

It appears most politicians are more interested in their own personal agenda rather than what's best for our country. Is that the way it is?

Now these fellows in Washington wouldent be so serious and particular if they only had to vote on what they thought good for the majority of the people of the U.S. That would be a cinch. But what makes it hard for them is, every time a bill comes up they have things to decide that have nothing to do with the merit of the bill. The principal thing is, of course: What will this do for me personally back home? Politics and self-preservation must come first, never mind the majority of the people. A politician's thoughts are naturally on his next term more than on his country.

— 🤠 —
RELIGION IN POLITICS

Our founding fathers held very strong religious beliefs. Should these beliefs remain a part of our political system?

There never was a nation founded and maintained without some kind of belief in something. The one thing that was "absolutely" necessary to run a Country on, and that is Religion. Never mind what kind; but it's got to be something or you will fail at the finish. I don't think that any one religion is the religion. Which way you serve your God will never get one word of argument or condemnation out of me.

Should the church be involved in politics (after listening to politics Monday through Saturday)?

Now you would think: 'Well, that gives us Sundays without having to listen to any politics!'

Don't you believe it. That's when you get more politics than all the rest of the week combined. That's when the preachers start 'lectioneering.' They all start out by saying: The church should not enter into politics, but.' Then they try to show how in their case it is different; that they are not entering politics, they are just advising; that people are so flighty nowadays, that if they are not advised properly, why, they are apt to be led astray by the opposition.

Can you tell us why the Ten Commandments are so important?

Whoever wrote the Ten Commandments made 'em short. They may not always be kept, but they are understood. They are the same for all.

Illustration by Kelly Killough, copyright protected

If the Lord wanted us to know exactly how and where we come from, he would let us know in the first place. He didn't leave any room for doubt when he told you how you should act when you got here. His example and the commandments are plain enough. Start from there. Never mind going back any farther.

How important is a politician's religion to the average voter?

What do we care about a man's Religion, we don't want to be saved spiritually; we want to be dragged out of the hole financially.

CORRUPTION IN POLITICS

What party was a leading force in bringing corruption into politics?

Corruption is supposed to be a Republican measure, and they are supposed to have perfected it up to the high standard that it occupies today. It's really not new. It has been in existence for years, but mostly in a small way, and practiced by the minor politicians.

In fact, the Democrats were supposed to have started it in what was called Tammany Hall. But a good thing can't be restricted and is bound to spread. So the Republicans had their eyes open for all the new wrinkles that would help them stay on the U.S. pension list. So like everything else, they took it and improved on it and brought corruption up to the high standard that it is today.

Is one political party more corrupt than the other?

The Democrats and the Republicans are equally corrupt — it's only in the amount where the Republicans excel.

Do you expect corruption to become an issue in this election?

It's going to be hard to make an issue of corruption. It's like the poor; it's always been with us.

The voter doesn't seem to care about corruption. Why is that?

It's hard to get people to believe a thing as corruption, when it's something that has always been going on. These deals gradually come under the heading of legitimate campaign business. You promise something in return for something, whether it is a post office, or an oil well. It's what the lawyers call 'sharp practice.' So it's going to be awful hard to get people interested in corruption unless they can get some of it.

CHANGES IN POLITICS

What is the best way to bring about change in politics?

Trouble with politics, it breeds politics. So that makes it pretty hard to stamp out. The only way to do it is at the source. We got to get birth control among politicians.

Is there an alternative to the two-party system today?

You see, if we didn't have two parties, we would settle on the best man in the country, and things would run fine. But as it is now, we settle on the two most eager ones, and then fight over 'em.

4

POLITICS
– & –
MONEY

JACK WELLS

WEALTHY VS. LOW INCOME

There seems to be a widening gap between wealthy and low income people today. Why is that?

The difference between our rich and poor grows greater every year. Our distribution of wealth is getting more uneven all the time. A man can make a million and he is on every page in the morning. But it never tells who give up the million that he got. You can't get money without taking it from somebody.

President Thomas Jefferson was the most far-sighted Democrat and they named the Democratic Party after him. That is he was for the poor but was himself of the rich. Jefferson sitting up there on that hill believed in equality for all. But he didn't divide up the hill with any poor Democrats.

Is there one guiding principle that shows up during these times?

There is one rule that works in every calamity. Be it pestilence, war or famine, the rich get richer and the poor get poorer. The poor even help arrange it.

You see, there's not an unemployed man in the country that hasent contributed to the wealth of every millionaire in America. Everyone of us, that have anything, got it by the aid of these people.

There's more than a million persons in the country with more money than ever before, but there's ten million people who are poorer than ever. It's up to us to do something about it.

Washington must not forget who rules when it comes to a showdown.

Illustration by Jack Wells, Western artist

THE ECONOMY

Are the Democrats correct when they say today's economic problems are the fault of the Republicans?

Don't blame all the things that have been happening to us lately on the Republican Party. They are not smart enough to have thought 'em up!

So much talk is taking place about reducing government debt and balancing the budget. How does this work?

Now take the budget. Early in the year the President sends what they call the 'budget' to Congress. It takes the head of every department in Washington six months to think up that many figures. You see, you have a budget like you have a limit in a poker game. You are not supposed to go beyond it till at least an hour after the game has been started. So we won't run over the budget limit till about next month. When we do, it makes work for another department in Washington. You see, here is what Congress does. It votes mythical beans into a bag, then tries to reach in and pull real beans out.

By the way, the way they are raiding the Treasury now, there don't look like it will do anybody any good to get elected. What's the use running your head off to get to a table where the food has just been all eaten up? If I was an office seeker, I would kinder be doubtful whether there was enough in there left to pay my regular salary, much less what I wanted to run for office for in the first place.

Lord, the money we do spend on Government and it is not one bit better than the government we got for one third the money twenty years ago.

Side note: The following anecdote gives an indication on how Will approached budget issues especially when he had his "personal advisor" by his side.

Will's wife, Betty, was always trying to get him to stick to a budget. Will had a new project at their ranch he wanted done.

He said, "Blake, (he always used her maiden name when the topic was serious) we need a dam up in the canyon to keep that whole mountainside from sliding down on us."

Betty wanted to know how much that dam would cost. Will thought for a moment and then said … "about $25,000." That's when Betty put her foot down. "Will … we can't do it this year, it is not in our budget!"

Will looked at her for a moment … then left the room. When he returned some minutes later, he was grinning like a kid. "Blake, Monday morning you order a crew to get started on that dam. I'm leaving tomorrow. I just booked me a little lecture tour for $25,000. So now the dam is on this year's budget."

Rogers saw a potential problem, came up with a doable solution; then jumped on the 'Train of Action' and got it done.

How will the different political parties deal with the issue of unemployment in this year's elections?

Each political party has some plan of relieving the unemployed. Both parties have discovered that while these folks are not working, there is nothing in the Constitution to prevent them from voting.

Prosperity is a phrase bandied about quite freely by our politicians. How do you view the prosperity issue?

You can't lick this prosperity thing, even the fellow that hasn't got any is all excited over the idea.

At this time the economy seems to be moving right along. Is this an indication of continuing prosperity?

No nation in the history of the world was ever sitting as pretty. If we want anything, all we have to do is go and buy it on credit. So that leaves us without any economic problems whatever, except some day to have to pay for them. But we are certainly not thinking about that this early.

A government spokesman says their data and statistics shows we are better off now than at any time in our country's history. Can we believe him?

You will try to show us that we are prosperous, because we have more. I will show you where we are not prosperous, because we haven't paid for it yet.

This country right now is operating on a dollar down and a dollar a Week. It ain't taxes that is hurting this country; it's Interest.

Are things getting better?

You keep reading about things getting better, but most of the articles are written by folks that are doing well themselves.

This would be a great time for some man to come along that knew something.

Are you worried about inflation?

I've been accused of being worried over this inflation. I wasent worried, I was just confused. Now there is quite a difference. When you are worried, you know what you are worried about, but when you are confused, you don't know enough about a thing to be worried. But even my confusion is all over now.

Everybody I meet has explained this whole thing so clearly that now I am going around explaining it myself. You see, medical science has two ways of actually tracing insanity. One is if the patient cuts out paper dolls; and the other is if the patient says, Hey, listen, I will tell you what this economic business really means!

What is this inflation business about?

Oh, I don't know what it's all about, I don't know any more about this than an economist, and God knows, he don't know anything.

What's changed our lives?

Buying on credit, waiting for relief, Ford cars, too many Republicans, Notre Dame coaching.

Many people today are caught in a squeeze between trying to refinance their mortgages, renew their notes and afford the high cost of gasoline. What advice do you have for folks caught up in this state of affairs?

Every one of us out there in the land of sunshine and second mortgages, is hustling from bank to bank, trying to renew our notes. A man has to be careful nowadays, or he will burn up more gasoline trying to get a loan than the loan is worth.

What caused our economy to be in such a fragile condition?

Honest, as we look back on it now, somebody ought to have taken each one of us and soaked our fat heads. We bought everything under the sun, but where was our payments going to come from, if we lost our jobs?

Why, that had never entered our heads. Why should we lose our jobs? Wasent all our big men telling us things was even going to get better? Was our prominent men warning us? If we had had a 'prominent' man, he would have, but we dident have any.

Why are there so many mortgages being foreclosed on today?

There never was a time in our lives where the foreclosing of a mortgage was as timely as it is today. It almost comes as standard equipment with most homes and farms.

What brought this on?

The working classes didn't bring this on. It was the big boys themselves who thought the financial drunk was going to last forever. They over merged and over capitalized and over everything else. That's the fix that we're in now.

So the "big boys," including the politicians, have all been involved in creating this financial mess?

It looks like the financial giants of the world have bungled as much as the diplomats and politicians.

You see there is a lot of things these old boys have done that are within the law, but it's so near the edge that you couldn't slip a safety razor blade between their acts and a prosecution.

Can the economic problems be solved by making credit more available as advocated by some of the politicians?

Our only solution of relief seems to be to fix it so people who are in a hole through borrowing can borrow some more. Borrowing, that's what's the matter with the world today. If no individual or country could borrow a dime for five years that would be the greatest five-year plan ever invented.

I was raised on a cattle ranch and I never saw or heard of a ranchman going broke, only the ones who had borrowed money. You can't break a man that don't borrow; he may not have anything, but Boy! He can look the World in the face and say, I don't owe you Birds a nickel.

You can't break a man that don't borrow.

How long will the depression [recession] last?

The depression [recession] won't end till we grow a generation that knows how to live on what they got.

America is a great country, but you can't live in it for nothing.

— 🤠 —
BANKS

Is it your position that banks have been a part of our economic problems?

It's not from a personal view that I am for abolishing banks. It's just that I don't think these boys realize what a menace they are. As far as being good fellows, personally, well, I have heard old-timers talk down home in the Indian Territory, and they say that Jesse James, or the Dalton Boys, were the most congenial men of their day, too.

Illustration by Jack Wells, Western artist

If you notice, they are always trying to put through some kind of bill in Congress, but nobody ever puts through one to do something about bank interest. No, Sir, you couldn't do that, because then you are getting into the business of the boys that really hold the hoops while the jumping is going on.

Why does a person receive a low rate of interest on their savings, while having to pay a much higher rate when he borrows?

They limit a Savings Bank from paying you more than a few percent, but anything is legal if you are the one to do the borrowing.

Is there an immediate government bailout coming to help banks as well as individuals who have lost their home or farm?

See where Congress passed a 2 billion-dollar bill to relieve bankers' mistakes and lend to new industries. You can always count on us helping those who have lost part of their fortune, but our whole history records nary a case where the loan was for the man who had absolutely nothing. Our theory is to help those who can get along even if they don't need it.

— 🎩 —
BIG BUSINESS

There seems to be a great concern among the average American today that major corporations and special interest groups with their lobbyist have too much influence over our elected officials. What is the best way to remedy this kind of situation?

If we have senators and Congressmen in Washington that can't protect themselves against these lobbyists, we don't need to change our lobbies, we need to change our representatives.

Does big business have any influence over Congress when it comes to taxes?

Every time Congress starts to tax some particular industry, it rushes down with its main men, and they scare Congress out of it. As it is now, we are taxing everybody without a lobby.

*Can you give us an example of big businesses attitude
on regulation?*

Big business went to see the president and they said: "Quit trying to
reform us, and just give us a chance to recover." The President says:
"Can't you reform and recover, too?"

But Big Business answered: "No! We can't do anything with a cop
on every corner watching everything we do. Give us a chance to
recover first, and honest when we are able, we will reform.

*How did "Big Business" get so big in its influence and
financial dealings?*

It got big by selling its stocks and not by selling its products. No
scheme was halted by the government as long as somebody would
buy the stock.

Is there anything that can disrupt business?

Two things can disrupt business in this country. One is war and the
other is a meeting of the Federal Reserve Board.

— 🎩 —

OIL COMPANIES

*How do you envision dealing with the oil companies and the
excessive profits they have reaped off the American public?*

Gasoline was never much higher. But there you have a business
that is in the hands of a few men, and they see that the price is
kept up. It's not regulated by supply and demand, it's regulated
by manipulation.

No business in the U.S. is as cockeyed as the oil business. If ever
a business needed a dictator, it is them. It would be the biggest
job held by a single man, outside the president. It must not be an
oilman, for he is already linked with one side or the other. It's got to

be a man that the whole oil industry knows is on the level, fearless, fair, seeking nothing but justice for thousands that produce oil, and millions that use it.

You remember, a few years ago, this country had to pass a special law called the Anti-Trust Law, aimed primarily at two trusts: the Oil and the Steel. Now, if you have to pass a law to curb businesses like that, they are not exactly the businesses to inspire confidence to the rest of the nation, in regard to keeping the law.

How do we reduce our dependence on oil and gasoline, and also eliminate the traffic congestions in our cities?

Pass a law that only paid-for cars be allowed to use the highways.

Do oil company's work in the best interest of consumers by operating ethical businesses?

Frank Phillips, of oil fame, was out the other day and said he was going to Washington. The oil men were going to draw up a code of ethics. Everybody present had to laugh. If he had said the gangsters of America were drawing up a code of ethics, it wouldn't have sounded near as impossible.

WALL STREET

Can you tell us how the New York Stock Exchange works to buy and sell stocks?

They stand and yell and sell something they haven't got, and buy something they will never get.

Mr. Rogers, what advice would you give today's investor who's considering the stock market as an investment?

Every nation must have its legalized form of gambling. We have our Wall Street.

Illustration by Jack Wells, Western artist

Don't gamble. Take all your savings and buy some good stock, and hold it until it goes up, then sell it. If it don't go up, don't buy it.

The government has taken action to bail out certain Wall Street firms. Is this a worthy cause?

[At one time] We couldn't spell a billion dollars, much less realize it, count it, or anything. But now, as a nation, we learn awful fast, till it won't be long now and we'll be working on the word trillion — that follows billion. You'll read: 'Congress has been asked to appropriate 2 trillion dollars to relieve the descendants of a race of people called 'Wall Streeters.'' This is a worthy cause and no doubt this small appropriation will be made, after all, they ARE the wards of the government.

I tell 'em that this Country is bigger than Wall Street, and if they don't believe it, I show 'em the map.

5

POLITICS
— & —
THE WORLD

FOREIGN AFFAIRS

How effective are America's Foreign Policies?

Americans have one particular trait that they need never have any fear of some other nation copying, and that is we are the only people that will go where we know we are absolutely not wanted.

America means well, we mean better than any country in the world, but we just seem to come out wrong. We send men and money and everything. For a so-called smart nation, I believe we can be the biggest yaps sometimes. And the funny thing is America never enters anything with any thought of gain. It's just as well that we don't.

Are we not doing the right things?

Now if there is one thing that we do worse than any other nation, it is try and manage somebody else's affairs.

America can carry herself and get along in pretty fair shape, but when she stops and picks up the whole world and puts it on her shoulders she just can't 'get it done.'

If we can just let other people alone and let them do their own fighting. When you get into trouble 5,000 miles from home, we've got to have been looking for it.

No matter what we do, we are wrong. If we help a nation, we are wrong. If we don't help 'em, we are wrong. There just ain't any such animal as International Good Will. It just lasts till the money you lent 'em runs out.

All America has to do to get in bad all over the world is just to start out on what we think is a Good Samaritan mission.

But shouldn't these foreign countries have democratic elections like us?

"When we start out trying to make everybody have 'moral' elections, why, it just don't look like we are going to have enough Marines to go round.

Illustration by Jack Wells, Western artist

I don't care how little your country is, you got a right to run it like you want to. When the big nations quit meddling, then the world will have peace.

What's the answer?

We will never have true civilization until we have learned to recognize the rights of others.

Somebody is always telling us in the papers how to prevent war. There is only one way in the World to prevent war, and that is, for every nation to tend to its own business.

When it comes to protecting America's Foreign interest, where do we begin?

America has a great habit of always talking about protecting American interests in some foreign country. Protect them here at home! There is more American interests right here than anywhere.

What is the difference between politicians and soldiers?

Ain't it funny how many hundreds of thousands of soldiers we can recruit with nerve. But we can't find one politician in a million with backbone.

Is there any good that comes from war?

One good thing about wars, it takes smarter men to figure out who loses 'em than it does to start 'em.

A sure certainly about our Memorial Days is, as fast as the ranks from one war thin out the ranks from another take their place. Prominent men run out of Decoration Day speeches, but the world never runs out of wars. People talk peace, but men give their life's work to war. It won't stop till there is as much brains and scientific study put to aid peace as there is to promote war.

You can't say civilization don't advance ... for in every war they kill you in a new way.

DIPLOMATS

Mr. Rogers, what is your perception of a diplomat's job?

A Diplomat's job is to make something appear what it ain't. A diplomat tells you what he don't believe himself, and the man he's tellin' it to don't believe him, so it balances. Diplomats meet and eat, then rush out and wire their Government they've completely fooled the other fella.

It seems the American people may have been misled by our diplomats or leaders as to the reasons for going to war against another country. Is this a good strategy to build credibility among your citizens?

It always helps out in your recruiting and your patriotism if you can make your own people believe you was the one pounced on. I think the only real diplomacy ever performed by a diplomat is in deceiving his own people after their dumbness has got them into a war.

You regard Dwight Morrow as one of our best diplomats, why?

Morrow was different; he recognized that the only way for people to get along was to be honest and tell each other what they think and get to understand one another.

AUTOMOBILES

Does the automobile contribute to the overall well being of our citizens?

Henry Ford has run over more people in one month then were killed in the Revolutionary and Civil War.

Now right here in the paper is the following: 'Annual Auto Bill of U.S. is 14 billion dollars.' In another part of the paper it tells that 22,000 met their death last year by auto. Fourteen billion dollars we paid to kill 22,000. About $635,000 apiece, with no charge at all for the wounded. THEY will run at LEAST two or three times as many as the killed, and for what? Why, just to get somewhere a little quicker — if you get there at all. If cholera or smallpox or some disease killed, or left affected that many, why, Congress and every agency of the government would be appropriating money and doing every mortal thing necessary to do something about it. But, as it is, we go right on.

We are the first nation in the history of the world to go to the poorhouse in an automobile.

— 🤠 —
HEALTH CARE

There's a great deal of concern over health care today especially as the pharmaceutical companies, with government support, promote ongoing streams of medications to treat both old and new diseases and maladies; diseases unheard of many years ago. Can it be that we Americans are not as healthy as our parents were?

In the old days, when we wasent sanitary, why, we were strong enough to withstand the germs. But nowadays, we have to be careful of the microbes, for if they get a hold on us, we are goners. We are not physically able to withstand 'em. In the old days, as many as wanted to could drink out of one cup, and the last one would just shake his head and swallow down microbes just as fast as they would accumulate. But now, the old individual cup won't go for over one sitting, or it will knock the second individual right into the infested class.

The old-fashioned gourd that the whole family drank out of, from birth till death, would kill more of the modern population than a war. We just ain't built to stand the assaults and batteries of an unwrapped-in-paper container. New handkerchiefs, everything is bundled up separately. Nothing comes by the gross anymore.

But while we have lost in strength and endurance, we have gained in amusement and instruction. For there is not an hour of any day that some one on the air don't keep us warned of what lies in wait for us in case we don't use their remedy. There is just more different things that can happen to us than there used to be.

NATURAL RESOURCES

What is your perception of how quickly we are using up our natural resources?

You know, Americans have been getting away pretty soft up to now. Every time we needed anything, why, it was growing right under our noses. Every natural resource in the world, we had it.

… the good Lord has sure been good to us. Now what are we doing to warrant that good luck any more than any other nation? Just how long is that going to last? Now the way we are acting, the Lord is liable to turn on us any minute; and even if He don't, our good fortune can't possibly last any longer than our natural resources.

EDUCATION

Issues within our educational system today plus the high cost of education, are forcing our educators to become so involved in filling out government forms they have gotten away from the real goal of education. How do you respond to that?

One of these days they are going to remove so much of the punk and hooey and the thousands of things that the schools have become clogged up with, and we will find that we can educate our broods for about one-tenth the price, and at the same time learning 'em something they might accidentally use after they escaped.

But us poor old, dumb parents, we just string along, and do the best we can, and send 'em as long as we are able, because we want them to have the same handicaps the others have, We don't know what it's all about, we just have to take the teachers' word.

They all think that education is our salvation, but you could turn ten college presidents loose in a forest, with nothing to eat, or nothing to get it with, and then ten old so-called ignorant backwoodsmen, and your presidents wouldn't last a week. The smarter a nation, the more wars it has. The dumb ones are too smart to fight. Our schools teach us what the other fellow knows, but it don't teach us anything new for ourselves. Everybody is learning just one thing, not because they will know more, but because they have been taught that they won't have to work if they are educated. Well, we have so many educated now that there is not enough jobs for educated people. Most of our work is skilled and requires practice, and not education.

But none of these big professors will come out and tell you that our education might be lacking, that it might be shortened, that it might be improved. They know as it is now that it's a racket, and they are in on it. You couldn't get me to admit that making movies was the bunk, either. None of us will talk against our own graft. We all got us our "rackets" nowadays. There is just about as much hooey in everything as there is merit. The heathens live with less effort, and less worry. Trying to live "past" our parents, and not "up to 'em" is one of our drawbacks. The old Chinese got the right idea along that line.

Anyhow, this education is just like everything else. You got to judge it by results. Here we are, better educated — according to educational methods — than we ever were, and we are worse off than we ever were. So it's not living up to its billing. It's over-rated, it's not worth the price. In fact, it's costing us more than it's worth. They got to devise some way of giving more for the money. All they are getting out with now is 'credits' and nobody on the outside is cashing 'em.

Speaking of education, does education make a difference in whether a candidate is a Republican, a Democrat or more ethical?

The more education he gets the less apt he is to be a Democrat and if he is very highly educated he will see the apple sauce in both parties.

Education never helped morals. The smarter the guy the bigger the rascal.

Mr. Rogers, did you ever go to college?

I could have gone to West Point, but I was too proud to speak to a Congressman.

Well, how do you feel about college?

College is wonderful because it takes the children away from home just as they reach the arguing stage.

CHAMBER OF COMMERCE & ILLEGAL IMMIGRATION

How has the Chamber of Commerce contributed to the illegal immigration problem?

The minute a fellow gets into the Chamber of Commerce he quits mowing his own grass.

If millionaires in the country would just go to work, why we wouldent need any immigration for years.

CLOSING
REMARKS

CLOSING REMARKS

Mr. Rogers, in the unlikely event you are defeated at the polls, will you be able to congratulate the winner?

I think I can accept defeat in as poor English, and with as well hidden 'sour grapes' as anyone you could have chosen.

I have already got in my mind the message of congratulations to the winner, and am really anxious to hurry up and lose, just to see how it will look in print.

Do you feel the purpose for entering this campaign made a difference at all?

We went into this campaign to drive the Bunk out of politics. But our experiment, while noble in motive was a failure … Goodbye and Good Luck from the only cheerful loser in the race.

Mr. Rogers, is there anything I can do for you this political season?

Will you do me a favor? If you see or hear of anybody proposing my name humorously, or semiseriously, for any political office, will you maim said party, and send me the bill. I not only don't 'choose' to run, I will say I won't run! No matter how bad the country will need a comedian by that time.

Do you have any final words of wisdom for our voters?

My word is good, and the other feller's ought to be, too.

[Remember] We are here just for a spell and then pass on. So get a few laughs and do the best you can. Live your life so that whenever you lose, you are ahead.

SUMMARY

WILL ROGERS embraced life. He utilized his natural gifts and talents to benefit others. While presenting simple, honest, powerful messages, he sprinkled them with his timeless values and principles.

Will's message helped countless folks who needed hope, inspiration, courage, as well as a few laughs to deal with the problems and issues of their day. Through stories, humor and commentary, his observations had a tremendous impact upon all people.

Will made a difference by modeling who he really was. His wit, wisdom and philanthropy will be remembered for generations to come whether it pertains to politics, business or life.

Will Rogers personified the phrase of "you've got to "Cowboy Up" when it's time to meet your responsibilities. It's time to honor your commitment, stand on your principles and make the choice to do the right thing!

If you like what you've read, please tell everyone you know I would really appreciate their support. Remember what Will said,

Life is not perfect and neither is politics.

Thank You!

ABOUT THE AUTHOR

— 🤠 —

I am just an old country boy in a big town trying to get along. I have been eating pretty regular, and the reason I have been is because I have stayed an old country boy.

— Will Rogers

CHARLEY'S TRAVELS have taken him from the eastern farm hills of Kansas, to military service, college administration as well as forays into the real estate and transportation industries. Other stops along the way included appearances in local TV commercials, movies plus recording radio advertisements for the Better Horses Network. Those various journeys provided a wealth of experience, a bit of wisdom and many lessons to draw on for his books as well as his current role as a professional entertainer and part-time cowboy.

Charley's a lot like Will Rogers in his story telling striving to take a common sense approach with a dash of humor tossed in when talking and writing about life's journeys. His stories range from the inspirational, humorous and motivational with some personal commentary added to the mix. Charley confesses to being a, "Professional Writer and Life Long Dreamer."

Recently he's added a few Country & Western songs along with some Cowboy Poetry all of which unexpectedly created a new brand when folks began referring to him as, "Cowboy Charley." His enriching, entertaining programs are certain to bring a smile to those in attendance.

To schedule Charley for an entertaining presentation to your organization on Will Rogers for President, e-mail him at CharleyGreen@CharleyGreen.com

www.CharleyGreen.com

Cartoon by Kevin Gritzke

RECOMMENDED READING
– & –
THE WILL ROGERS MEMORIAL MUSEUM

THE QUOTABLE WILL ROGERS
By Joseph H. Carter
Gibbs Smith Publisher, Layton, Utah

NEVER MET A MAN I DIDN'T LIKE
The Life And Writings Of Will Rogers
By Joseph H. Carter
Avon Books, New York.

THE BEST OF WILL ROGERS
By Bryan Sterling
M. EVANS & COMPANY, INC., New York

WILL ROGERS, A BIOGRAPHY
By Ben Yagoda
University of Oklahoma Press, Norman, OK

WILL ROGERS MEMORIAL MUSEUM
1720 West Will Rogers Blvd.
Claremore, OK 74017
(800) 324-9455 www.WillRogers.com

The museum is a special treat, displaying memories and the history of Will Rogers in impressive surroundings. Plan to make a trip to this wonderful museum honoring one of America's heroes, who stepped up when the nation called. Tell them Charley told you to stop by.

To support this candidacy and learn more about Will's views and philosophy relating to current issues, purchase one or more copies of:

Will Rogers for President	$9.95 per copy + $3.00 S&H
Audio Book (CD) also available	
Will Rogers on Elections & Politics	$9.95 per copy + $3.00 S&H
Will Rogers & Charley	$9.95 per copy + $3.00 S&H

Purchase all three for only $24.95 + $5.00 S&H
at www.CharleyGreen.com

For quantity discounts contact CharleyGreen@CharleyGreen.com.
www.CharleyGreen.com

All of the above products are also available from the Will Rogers Memorial Museum, www.WillRogers.com

View YouTube video clips of insightful interviews featuring Charley Green presenting many of Will Rogers' Thoughts, Quotes & Anecdotes On Important Election Issues

E-Books are available at CharleyGreen.com, Barnes & Nobel, Sony, Apple, Smashwords or Amazon.com

How to Promote YOUR Business with Books

1. As a gift to prospective customers.
2. Give a book to people or organizations who can refer business to you.
3. As a bonus for responding to an advert or direct mail offering.
4. Send book to your customers at year's end, thanking them for their business.
5. Use as a thank you for a sales appointment.
6. Mail a book to your prospect list to stay in touch with them.
7. Use them as a Christmas card — the cover can be overprinted.
8. Offer a book as a bonus if someone replies to a time sensitive offer.
9. Offer as a bonus for a sale over a certain size.
10. Give the book away at a trade show to attract more prospects to your stand.
11. Give as an incentive for completing a Customer Survey Form.
12. Include a book as a "Thank You" for the order, when sending an invoice or statement.
13. Bundle or package several book as a value added bonus for ordering a particular product.
14. Use as prizes in a raffle or charity event.
15. Give a book to the first 50 people who come into your shop or business.
16. Use a book to launch a new product including product details in the center of the Booklet.
17. Use a book as a memorable change of address.

www.ingramcontent.com/pod-product-compliance
Lightning Source LLC
Chambersburg PA
CBHW071022040426
42443CB00007B/893